The Scent of a Woman

The Scent of a Woman

"EVERY WOMAN HAS A SCENT BY
WHICH SHE IS DISTINGUISHED.
WHAT IS YOURS?"

PAMELA ODOM

To order additional copies of this book, contact:
Xlibris
1-888-795-4274
www.Xlibris.com
Orders@Xlibris.com
714016

Contents

I dedicate this book to my daughter, Jordan, and in memory of my mother, Ella Mae Mccaskill.

Jordan, the scent of beauty exudes from you. You are God's love at its best. Know your worth always. And do not allow yourself to be reduced to the opinions of no one. Love and trust God with all your heart, and with him, you can conquer and rise above anything.

And to my mom, who somehow, out of all she wasn't, became all that she could to give me all that I have. It was through you, Mom, that I learned that the scent of a woman was the strength of a woman and that Ella was her name.

Acknowledgment

I would like to thank my husband, Michael, who tirelessly and selflessly supports me and my dreams. He does a very fine job at making sure they all come true. I love you. You are my hero. I am a better woman because of you.

To my amazing three: Michael II, Christopher Michael, and my daughter, Jordan Noelle, who makes me feel as if I can conquer the world.

I would like to thank my dream team: Charday Felder, Yolonda Hunt, Joevornia Rodgers, Shelley Silverman, and Ashley Smith. There's a reason why there's five of you. God sent me grace to uphold and sustain me as I was writing this book.

Introduction

It is my hope that what I share in this book will encourage and empower you to get in touch with who you really are; to fight back; to know your worth and not to not settle for anything less than what you deserve; to learn from mistakes; to get back up once or if you have fallen; more importantly, to not blame others for your stuff; to take responsibility for your choices and actions and grow through it; to go back and get some of the things that someone may have taken from you and perhaps walked away with; to encourage you not to get stuck in your pain; to forgive yourself and anyone else who may have caused that pain; to own it, cry over it, and then let it go, believing that God has greater for you.

Now, it is important that you intentionally soul-search as you read this book. Are you happy and fulfilled or broken and shattered? Are you attracting what you're giving off—whether good bad or indifferent? Could the scent that's emanating from you be the reason for some losses and pain in your life? For example, why were you chosen as the girlfriend but not as the wife? What has not been resolved in you that you keep pushing people away? Is it the scent of promiscuity caused by sexual abuse? Is it the scent of insecurity caused by abandonment? Is it the scent of sexual confusion caused by rejection? Or perhaps, you are good and you are reading this that you may be of help to someone else.

Either way, through the words I share in this book, you may be able to get some insight as to whether your scent is repellent or attractive. *Are you fine eau de parfum or eau de toilette?* Fine *parfum* means that you know your value and your worth. Cheap toilette, well, that explains itself.

Chapter 1

The Scent of a Woman

There is nothing more beautiful to see than seeing a woman who is sure of herself—not conceited, but confident; sound in her thinking; and strong in her stand; vulnerable, but not weak. She makes a statement without uttering a word. Her presence fills a room like a sweet-smelling aroma. She does not even desire the attention, but it can't be helped. Her scent announces her!

The scent of a woman is the odor she gives off, by which she is perceived. Therefore, she is identified by what she smells like. What's emanating from her is usually what's going on inside of her. That scent is either heightened or diminished based on her self-perception—what she believes or perceives about herself. So with that being said, I leave you with these questions: What do you smell like? What is your scent?

We all know that when a woman gets dressed, she tops her outfit off with her favorite fragrance.

Fragrance is like the cherry-on-top of a perfect outfit. It adds a sensory layer to your look, conveys an attitude or mood, and reflects your unique personality. Many people select a 'signature scent' and wear it all the time, hoping the scent will identify them as soon as they walk into a room. Sometimes people wear that same scent forever; sometimes they change it as the mood strikes. Either way, it comes down to this: Everyone wants to smell good.

Have you ever noticed, though, that some of the fragrances you wear seem to last a long time, and others seem to dissipate almost immediately? You might think you're just not putting on enough fragrance, but that's actually not the case.

There are several reasons why some fragrances last and others don't (skin, concentration, and notes). You can experiment to find out which one might be your issue and make changes.

Your skin. If you have dry skin, you probably don't have the necessary oils for the perfume to be absorbed into your skin. Therefore, the fragrance will evaporate faster. Try applying unscented moisturizer before applying your fragrance. Or you can try "layering" scents if your favorite fragrance also comes in a shower wash or body lotion variety.

Concentration. Perfumes come in various concentrations. The higher the concentration, the more fragrant, and the longer the scent will last (meaning the perfume contains more oils than alcohol). For example, an eau de parfum will always be more concentrated than an eau de toilette. A body spray would be much less concentrated than an eau de toilette. Remember, though, that concentrations vary among product lines. Generally, the more alcohol in the scent, the faster it will lose its scent.

Notes. Notes are what make up a fragrance. Most fragrances have top, middle, and base notes. These notes are scents with different molecular weights that develop at different rates when applied to the skin. Top notes are the first you smell in a perfume. They evaporate more quickly than the rest of the scents.

The middle notes are the "body" of the perfume and take longer to develop on the skin than top notes. The base notes are the final scent to develop and last the longest. They're also a fixative that slows down the evaporation of the top and middle notes, making the overall scent last longer. The stronger the base note, the longer the fragrance lasts. Some cheap fragrances don't even bother with base notes, and unsurprisingly, they don't last long at all.

Your scent can be the reason for what's right or very wrong in your life. As you can see a fragrance is only as powerful as the ingredients that it is made up of. What fragrance are you adorning yourself with on a daily basis. How substantial is the content? Is what you've personally invested in having a temporary or long lasting affect? The scent that emanates from a woman says a lot about who she is and why she may do what she does. For example, you can't seem to attract the right man to love when all you have is love to give. Or you can get the guy but can't keep him—good enough to date but not to marry. What are you made up of that causes you to smell the way you do or that causes people to respond or not respond to you the way that they do. What is your scent saying about you, that is the question?

Here's a story about a girl.

How would a woman be perceived if she goes to her ex-boyfriend's wedding, (not formally invited) catches the bouquet at the reception, and dares to take pictures with him and his new bride? Well, we know *crazy* would probably be the perception. However, an even better question would be, who does that and, more importantly, why? What was going on within her that would cause her to do such a thing? One would guess, out of control emotions. For as we know our emotions have a way of making a fool out of us at some point or another.

And yes, foolish I was. I really don't know why I did that. Perhaps disbelief. I was the church girl who, for five years, dated the church boy who married another girl. And probably what was going on inside of me was emotional distress. I am not sure. Perhaps too immature to understand and not grounded enough in God to get the revelation. I was only eighteen-years old.

I look back on it now with great shame—more so because I was selfishly engulfed in my own emotions that I gave no thought to how my presence at their wedding made his wife feel. Ladies, we should never be so self-indulgent that we're not considerate of how our actions may affect our sisters.

Having now matured over the years, I believe that if we can get to the root of some of our unanswered whys, some of these foolish actions would not occur. And we won't have forty and fifty year old women acting as I did back then, as an eighteen year old. Now I must add right here that loving and losing someone is not the worst thing in the world. In fact, sometimes it's the best thing, because we don't always know how in our immaturity, to let go of what's not for us. So, our hands have to be forced.

The pain doesn't always allow you to see it at the time, but trust me; you will eventually see it—just as I did. God healed me, and matured me, thus changing my scent. He then strategically placed me in a position where my changed scent would attract my now husband (of twenty-eight years), whom I married him six months after having met him. God had a plan. So please be encouraged to know that God knows what's best for us. And the losses that he allows are really set ups for greater gain. Praise God!

Although at eighteen years of age that was a lot of emotions to deal with, it was a great life lesson. I've come to this resolve, that there are three must-haves you must have. These three things will keep you grounded in the face of emotional distress.

1. *A relationship with God.* Having God helps you to not be like the silly women Timothy speaks of in 2 Timothy 3:6, but to be like the woman mentioned in Titus 2 who is sober; grave; temperate; sound in faith, charity, and patience; and able to teach the younger women. The book of Proverbs, in chapter 31, describes a virtuous woman as: moral, principled, and ethical.

   With God, all things are possible, for he is the keeper of our souls—our mind, will, and emotions.

2. *Self-fulfillment.* What is self-fulfillment? Self-fulfillment is the act of fulfilling one's desires through one's own efforts. Why self-fulfillment? Every woman needs something that she can call her own. If not, she would be trying to

identify who she is by comparing her life to the lives of other women. Even if she has a family, it is not enough, especially if she's everything to everybody and nothing to herself. It's like the housewife; she cares for her husband and children, and then when the children come of age and move out, she is lost. Or if the marriage or relationship fails for any reason, she ends up having to start life all over again, feeling void of purpose and no longer able to identify who she is. If you haven't done so already, be intentional about being whole and taking care of yourself. A fulfilled woman is a more complete and effective woman.

3. *Courage.* Courage gives you strength in the face of fear. It will help you make the hard decisions. And it will keep you from holding on to the things and/or the people that you should be letting go. Having courage makes you more apt to do or pursue things that you otherwise would not. Courage gives you the strength to keep showing up even against the odds. What would have happened if Hannah

didn't have the courage to keep showing up at the house of the Lord to pray for God to open her womb?

As she continued praying before the Lord, Eli observed her mouth.

Hannah was speaking in her heart; only her lips moved, and her voice was not heard. Therefore, Eli took her to be a drunken woman. And Eli said to her, "How long will you go on being drunk? Put your wine away from you." But Hannah answered, "No, my lord, I am a woman troubled in spirit. I have drunk neither wine nor strong drink, but I have been pouring out my soul before the Lord. Do not regard your servant as a worthless woman, for all along I have been speaking out of my great anxiety and vexation." Then Eli answered, "Go in peace, and the God of Israel grant your petition that you have made to him." And she said, "Let your servant find favor in your eyes." Then the woman went her way and ate, and her face was no longer sad. (1 Samuel 1:10–20)

So, if you're lacking courage in an area in your life (e.g., courage to speak up for yourself, courage to leave an abusive relationship, courage to make a career change), whatever it may be, ask God to grant you courage. Without it, some things in your life will never change. If you want favorable results, do as Hannah did—take courage and keep showing up in the face of God even when people are talking because they are privy to the facts about your deficiencies, laughing and perhaps judging and questioning the validity of your relationship. It is in the position of prayer that you will see the hand of God move in your life. So, take courage and maintain your position.

Now after gathering this information about how scents and fragrances are developed, I felt the need to spiritualize it so one could make it personally applicable.

Let's say that your faith is the fragrance and is made up of three notes: top note, middle note, base note. Believing is the top note. Trusting is the middle note. And knowing is the bottom note. Now these three notes carry three different weights. Believing gets you to the door. Trusting gets you to open the door. Knowing gets you to walk through the door. The stronger the base note (your knowing), the longer the fragrance (your faith) lasts. The more you know, the stronger your faith is.

After having read the above descriptions, *where do you find yourself?* Do you exude an eau de parfum or a eau de toilette?

Chapter 2

The Power of Scent

Anything or anyone who has power has the capacity or ability to influence the behavior of others or the course of events. In other words, anything that has the ability to produce an effect has power.

In this chapter, I am referring to the power that a scent carries. A scent can be so powerful that it can attract or repel. It can be a turn-on or a turn-off. It will brighten your day or make you sick to your stomach. Think about it. "What is that smell?" has two meanings. What is your response to a woman in your presence who smells good versus one who does not smell so good?

It is also so powerful that it even correlates with memory. You can smell a scent that will immediately bring back memories, whether good or bad, of a time in your life or of a relationship or of a location. So, with all that being said, I can't help but think about this information that I had come across during my research.

Did you know that male animals mate or search for their potential female mates based on her scent?

Read further.

Reference: (news.bbc.co.uk/earth/hi/earthnews/newsid) In fading light, a male meadow vole moves past a female and catches the whiff of her fragrance. The scent catches his attention. He turns, sensing she may be the one he has spent his life searching for. He follows her trail, eager to impress.

What he has detected in these few moments—from this haze of pheromones [pheromones are airborne chemical messengers released from the body that have a physical or emotional effect on another member of the same species]—is not that the female is his soul mate, a potential life partner, or someone to captivate his mind. But that she is a virgin. By her scent he is able to smell whether a potential female partner is a virgin, and if not, how many times she's mated.

It seems that the males use scent as an indicator and that virgin females smell very different from those that have had multiple partners because they produce very different chemicals. Footnote: (BBC, website "Earth News.")

Wow! I thought to myself.

Immediately I thought about human male-female relationship. And even further, I thought about the biblical teachings on sexual morality and abstinence and why it's necessary. Could the premature indulgence or overindulgence then be the cause of some woman's loneliness and unfulfillment? Could it be that because of this, the ability to attract the right mate has diminished?

I then came across some research by biologist Dr. Melissa Thomas of the University of Western Australia, Crawley, who has published the latest review how some male species can actually apply chemicals to females while mating with them—sneakily rubbing on perfumes that deter rivals from later mating with "their" female.

I was wowed again. And it's probably more so because the research says that the male "sneakily" rubs perfumes to deter rivals, which brought me to

"Who left a scent on you that has caused you to be undesirable to someone else?" Think about it. Are your chemical messengers tripping you up? Who took away the beauty of who you were created to be? Who took ownership of you without your permission?

I raise these questions to make you think, because sometimes we are not aware of how we have really been affected by the actions of someone that we have given our souls to. You really don't know how deeply rooted the bitterness or pain is until you start digging. So, keep digging. It's time to change your scent.

Chapter 3

What Do You Smell Like When It's Not Your Fault?

We as women are good at hiding or masking what's really going on within us. But there's one thing that we cannot mask; that is the scent that emanates from us. Good, bad, or indifferent—it exudes.

What do you smell like? What statement does your presence make? How sure of yourself are you? Do you shrink in certain crowds? What about your self-esteem? Do you have confidence in your self-worth and abilities? Do you have any sore spots or wounds that have not healed? Have you been rejected and now, out of fear, you're unsure about who and what to accept? Are you angry? Do you have any open-ended situations that need closure? Have you had all the necessary conversations with the people that you need to have them with?

Wherever you may find yourself in the questions above, it is what your scent is made up of and what you may smell like.

When It's Not Your Fault

When we are born, we are born to life with our hearts and minds in their purest form. We are then molded by the environment that we are born into or placed into. Either we become wholesome, thriving little girls, teens, and then adults, or we become fragmented, dysfunctional little girls, teens, and then adults.

Our scent is therefore developed as a result of the environment that we've been dwelling in.

It's so crazy how things get attached to us, having nothing to do with the blood line but rather the environment we were or are placed into. Unfortunately, sometimes the environment is unhealthy and not conducive to wholeness, thus breaking us. And since we are molded by our environments, it is in those places that we lose our self-worth, self-esteem, and even identity—e.g., being left with someone you should be able to trust like a babysitter or a family member or family friend or even a sick-minded spiritual leader and taken advantage of physically or emotionally and even sexually.

As a result, you grow up trying to fulfill a feeling and desire that you really don't understand because you were exposed to it prematurely. And now as an adult, you're not able to love, be loved, or give of yourself intimately without feeling violated because one of the most beautiful parts of love has become a dreadful nightmare—all because someone mishandled you, took advantage of your innocence, dropped you and left you crippled and not able to move about in life properly, and disabled and impaired you at no fault of your own.

So, what do you do when you have to overcome a personal traumatic experience that you didn't ask for? I am reminded of Jonathan's son in the Bible.

(Jonathan son of Saul had a son who was lame in both feet. He was five years old when the news about Saul and Jonathan came from Jezreel. His nurse picked him up and fled, but as she hurried to leave, he fell and became disabled. His name was Mephibosheth.) (2 Samuel 4:4, New International Version, NIV)

Now here in this story, you have a child who was dropped and crippled through no fault of his own. He was dropped not by just anyone but by a nurse who was trained to keep people well. And because of her emotional haste, he was then lame and could not walk. This biblical story is an example of someone suffering pain and loss at the hands of another. Now, of course, her intention was not to harm him. But because of her emotional state, she did.

How do you get over the emotional scars that are inflicted upon you by the emotionally wounded—scars and disabilities that prevent you from moving effectively through life? Although this may be challenging it's possible. Did you not know that your disability had privileges? God has a way of taking disabilities that hinder and turning them into privileges that heal.

Because of Mephibosheth's disability, he had the honor of being able to sit and eat daily at the king's table. Your disabilities and inabilities usher you into the presence of the king. And how do you not get healed sitting and eating in the presence of the king?

Another example is being raised motherless or fatherless because you were the product of an affair or born to a single parent. So it's possible that due to not being nurtured by your mother, you have not gotten the proper care and attention you needed to know what unconditional love is. Therefore, you don't know how to give it or receive it, or you haven't been affirmed by your father; therefore, you grow up not knowing who you really are, and you feel incomplete, so you are then defined by who people say you are.

You end up searching for people and things to fill a void. You have unanswered questions, and not too many things seem sure or safe. In one environment, you feel as if you can conquer the world, but in others, you feel vulnerable, as if the world has conquered you. Your life is like a puzzle with missing pieces. You can never really appreciate the beauty of what that picture is until you fill in the missing pieces. So, then you're left with this question: how do I function normally outside of dysfunction when dysfunction is my normal?

Get Rid of the Sitting Garbage

This is not my fault! So, what do I do about it?

While the fact remains that you cannot do anything about the things that were not your fault or the things that are out of your control, there are some things that are in your control, so you must take action. It is in your control to make up your mind to be whole. It's all according to what you say and believe. It's a choice.

We sometimes try so hard to pretend that we're okay as a way of protecting ourselves when in actuality we're causing more damage to our emotional selves. Unforgiveness, bitterness, and pain are enemies of the soul, and if left not dealt with, these things will have you reeking of a bad smell, like sitting garbage left unattended. *Left unattended* means it sits and sits without being discarded, and God forbid if it's sitting in the heat; the smell is worse.

So it is with the stuff that we leave unattended in our lives. When the heat of life challenges is turned up, the scent of the unresolved issues of pain, through insecurity, low self-esteem, and even anger emanates.

The garbage has sat long enough. You must find the strength to get rid of it. I know it can be hard to do because you are afraid, and somehow holding on seems to give you a sense of security. However, dealing with the worse of who you are brings out the best of who you are. So confront it, deal with it, and let it go. It's time to turn that bad smell into a sweet-smelling aroma. No, it was not your fault, and you can be free from it. It can only have as much power as you give it.

Chapter 4

Five Ways to Change and Maintain Your Scent

Ways to Make Your Scent Last Longer

It's a *choice.*

It's all up to *you.* Do you not know that right now, in this moment, whether you are happy, sad, or indifferent is a result of the choices you have made?

I remember the day that "It's a choice" occurred to me.

I would often get offended by the actions of others, trying to make sense of why people do what they do. This particular day, I said, "I choose not to be offended." In that moment, my perspective about a lot of things changed. It was an amazing moment of freedom. So, from that day forward It's a choice became my new motto. So today make it your motto. Choose you. Choose freedom over bondage; chose not to succumb but rather to overcome; Choose the fragrance of beauty and wholeness.

Know Your Worth

What is your worth?

Your worth is your moral or personal value, and it is defined by what you think and believe about yourself, not by the opinions of others.

Knowing your worth brings you to an awareness about yourself that will eradicate every insecure feeling and need for validation. Your confidence and self-worth is so boosted that *fearfully* and *wonderfully* are not just words you repeat with wishful thinking but rather what you confidently come to know and live. You will be able to take a stand for yourself and not settle for anything less than what you deserve. Now I do understand that life happens and perhaps you were not so lucky; somewhere along the line, you lost yourself and need to get back to the essence of who you are.

"Somebody almost walked away with my stuff" is a quote from Loretta Devine in the movie *For Colored Girls* by Tyler Perry. Boy, did that resonate with me. I thought about the times I was hurt, mishandled, and/or misunderstood and what and where I could have been had I not come to know my worth. So, what does that statement actually mean? It means that the actions of another person could possibly strip you of your self-worth and leave you void of your value.

How many times in a relationship where you loved and lost and felt like you couldn't get anyone else because your confidence and your self-worth were shattered? The best of who you were was taken by someone who did not know how to handle you. You trusted and was betrayed, causing you to lose confidence in who you once believed you were. Think about it. In what relationship did you lose the essence of who you were? Where were you emotionally when you got robbed of your self-worth, self-esteem, and dignity? Identify that place, and go back and get your stuff.

Remember, you teach people how to treat you.

Things to Live By

1. You must first know that your worth is not determined by the opinion of others but rather by what you believe about yourself.

2. You do not allow people to reduce you to their ideology of what they think you should be.

3. Be sober because when you're not, you will operate from a drunken state. Sound decisions cannot be made with an unstable mind.

4. Let go of toxic relationships. Toxic relationships will eat away at the core of who you are and take away from your very existence. It will have you overindulging in and overcompensating for the wrong things and in areas that won't allow you to produce good fruit.

Do It Right Here, Lord!

It's a matter of the *heart*.

We all have a place, a "sore" spot, that only God knows about—a place that appears to be healed until it is touched. One morning, I was riding along in my car, communing with God. Some of my most intimate times with God has been and still is in my car. I'm sure you can identify with your car being a prayer room. I have cried, sung, and surrendered all my private thoughts and feelings—thoughts of ill will out of defense of myself and even personal insecurities. It was in those "real" private times that I got a release in my soul and was brought to a state of repentance.

So, one day while riding, I was thinking about how I have to stop giving power to fruitless situations and negative things that were attaching themselves to me and occupying my good headspace. So, I began to meditate and pray, yielding everything that was holding me emotionally captive. As the spirit began to make an intercession, in that moment, I began to wonder why some spots were still sore.

Was I really allowing myself to be healed? With questions front and center staring me in my face, I had to do some soul-searching to identify the root cause, which everyone must absolutely do if healing is desired. As I began to soul-search, I soon discovered that I didn't do well with betrayal, disrespect, or being misunderstood. And manipulators aggrieved my spirit. As a result, I developed trust issues; therefore, I shut myself down and out from those whom I felt meant me harm and I would even hold on to ill feelings, shamefully, for a while. In prayer, however, I was brought to repentance. I don't know what your sore spots are, but I want to admonish you to choose healing and be made whole. Be honest with yourself. Understand that before you can be your best self, you must first acknowledge your worst self.

Here's what I've done and still do every time I experience or feel any ill will rising in me.

I submit my will to God and invite him in by asking, "Do it right here, Lord." I lay my hand across my heart. It's an invitation for change. Who better to ask to protect your heart than God? Bear in mind Proverbs 4:23: "Guard your heart with all diligence for out of it flows the issues of life." I promise you, in that moment, freedom will come. Psalms 46 declares that God is our refuge and our strength—a very present help. Your conviction and submission will usher you into a real life-changing encounter with God.

Take the Leap

You will never know unless you try.

You will always know when God is trying to tell you something. He sends confirmation. Well, for me, it happened to be Steve Harvey with his "take the jump". When I first heard his clip on social media, I laughed in amazement at the similarity of the messages and said "I hear you, Lord" because I would say this all the time to women who were aspiring to do things like starting a business etc. . . and was too afraid to do so. Unlike me who "took the leap" afraid, and started a business with no money. Just faith. I spoke it as a saw it. And then pursued it until it manifested.

I closed my eyes and opened my heart to believe and my mind to receive, and when I took the leap, God caught me in midair and brought me to a safe landing. Now I cannot leave out that when I heard Steve Harvey's "Take the jump," I felt as if it was God's way of reminding me of what I would tell people quite often: "Take the leap," "You owe it to yourself," "You will never know unless you try," "You don't want to live your life wishing: I shoulda, coulda woulda."

I needed the reminder because here I was in a quandary as I was turning fifty and was given a trip to Marco Island, Florida (because I so wanted to go) and had to live up to my own words. I had to take the leap by conquering one of my greatest fears—flying!

I must add that taking the leap is not just about starting businesses or new ventures. Taking the leap could have everything to do with you walking away from unhealthy relationships—relationships that do not add to your life but rather take away. And sometimes you stay too long out of fear of being alone or the fear of the opinions of others. *Take the leap! Even if you have to take it scared.*

Move Forward, Never Backward

Don't look back; you're not going that way.

Forgetting those things that are behind and reaching forth unto those things that are before is what Paul writes in the book of Philippians. This must be the mind-set of anyone who is trying to move past anything in their lives, especially those things that have not proven to be fruitful.

And if what you let go is supposed to be a part of your destiny, it will meet you in your forward.

You must stay focused on the goal. Adopt the characteristics of the grasshopper; it only hops forward, never backward.

Three Representations of a Scent

There are three women in the Bible that come to mind as I conclude this chapter on changing and maintaining your scent as a sweet-smelling aroma: Jezebel, Leah, and Esther.

Jezebel: Scent of Manipulation

She's a manipulative woman—vile and vicious and offensive in character.

There's something about a woman who becomes weakened by her inner unfulfilled desires. The root of that unfulfilled desire produces a spirit of emotional manipulation, and if not dealt with, that spirit goes out of control—vile, vicious and offensive in character. It will seek someone to latch on to and control, hoping to receive some personal validation.

Don't be this woman! Don't be a manipulator!

Leah: Scent of Insecurity

The woman with no voice, Leah was a pawn used in someone else's deception. She was married to Jacob, whom she knew loved and wanted her sister. Leah was not the first choice. Can you imagine how it feels to be with a man whose body is with you but whose heart is with another woman? So it's like you're competing with a fantasy—his fantasy. You're having babies and making adjustments while losing yourself at the same time, trying to get him to love you.

Speak up! Don't be a woman without a voice!

Esther: Scent of Confidence

A woman with confidence does not wait for things to happen; she make things happen. Esther took it upon herself to sacrifice her life to save her family (the book of Esther, the second chapter). So, don't just be a woman of beauty but also a woman of character and substance, influence and action. Be confident of this, he who began a good work in you will carry it on to completion (Phillipians 1:6). Be this woman!

Chapter 5

The Victory Lap and the YES

A victory lap is a lap that you would take after you have participated in a race and won. You're winning would be predicated upon you agreeing to participate and then enduring the process that positions you to win.

So, what am I saying? Your victory is in your *yes*!

I remember being at a spiritual breaking point. God had me at a place where I would hear his voice ever so clearly: "When will you love me enough to deny yourself?" At that time in my life, every decision that I was making was about me and what I selfishly wanted. I was going to church and yet not whole. I knew what I needed to do, but I just didn't want to do it. The responsibility and accountability seemed greater than what I was willing to contend with, and besides, it would require me to get out of my comfort zone.

So, because of my disobedience, God allowed a Jonah experience to occur in my life (Jonah 1). I was swallowed up and consumed by betrayal. All my close relationships were under fire, and people whom I had trusted betrayed me. I was devastated. It was one unexpected pain after another. But somehow as uncertain as I felt, I felt that much more certain that what I was experiencing was necessary. And it wasn't until one night in a prostrate position on the bathroom floor that I realized that God had allowed this because he was repositioning me to shift me. He had to reposition me before the shift; otherwise, I would not have survived the shift. He allowed what I call the TRE experience—tribulation, revelation, elevation.

Tribulation. Tribulation somehow seems to get you back in tune with the feelings you've masked or ignored. It awakens that part of you that becomes desensitized to reality.

Revelation. Revelation is bringing to the light what you're seeing but not discerning. Once I had been awakened by tribulation, God had my attention. I was then able to spiritually see what was happening and why it was happening. The face-to-face betrayal and harsh reality was necessary to get me to detach. If not, I would have been holding on to what I should have been letting go of. Although we sometimes try, we cannot take everyone to our next level. Stop placing people in your life where they don't belong. Bear in mind that even an elevator has a weight capacity.

Elevation. The tribulation and revelation are really about preparation to ensure that you are not only ready but capable of handling the elevation. Elevation is about greater work. Greater worker requires greater insight and strength.

Pain has a way of pushing you into a complete *yes*. God will divinely interrupt your life to save your life. It was in my yielding, embracing, and surrendering that God granted me grace to overcome. Healing and freedom came to my soul (mind, will, emotions).

My scent now exudes an aroma of wholeness, and my freedom now attracts and draws other women out of their bondage.

In order for your scent to change, you must become immersed in the will of God for your life. It is in that immersion that transformation will take place. No longer was I just informed, but I was transformed, understanding that the immersion was necessary for me to have a fresh scent. You cannot put perfume on an unclean body, or else the scents will conflict.

All the aforementioned issues are the things that may have diminished your scent. You can take those life experiences and challenges and become effective or infectious. In other words, you can empower or contaminate. And if by chance you have been left broken, wounded, or dysfunctional as a result, your healing is in your yes. Yield, embrace and surrender to God without contingencies. Your yes changes your posture, your posture puts you in position, and it is in that position that you're able to hear clearly God's divine plan for your life.

This is what the Lord says: "When seventy years are completed for Babylon, I will come to you and fulfill my good promise to bring you back to this place. For I know the plans I have for you," declares the Lord, "plans to prosper you and not to harm you, plans to give you hope and a future. Then you will call on me and come and pray to me, and I will listen to you. You will seek me and find me when you seek me with all your heart. I will be found by you," declares the Lord, "and will bring you back from captivity. (Jeremiah 29:11–14)

In Christ, God leads us from place to place in one perpetual victory parade. Through us, he brings knowledge of Christ. Everywhere we go, people breathe in the exquisite fragrance.

Because of Christ, we give off a sweet scent rising to God, which is recognized by those on the way of salvation—an aroma redolent with life (2 Corinthians 2:15–16). Your *yes* brings you into alignment and connects you to God. Your yes is the lifeline. It allows for an exchange, a spiritual transfusion, to take place. It's like tainted blood being replaced by new blood. The new blood gives you a new lease on life. Your yes is your yielding, embracing, and surrendering all to God without inhibitions. Having no inhibitions do not necessarily mean having no fear. And fear does not mean it's not possible.

So say *yes*! Through your submission to God, your scent changes. He extends his grace and clothes you with his love. And we all know that there's something special about the way a man loves a woman. When he loves her right, it absolutely brings out the best in her. The best of who she is rises to the top, and the fragrance of beauty and desirability emanates from her.

God will take the worst of who you were—your secrets, your lies and the lies that you believed in that made you do what you did, your indiscretions, and bad decisions—and clean you up and give you a sweet-smelling, undisputed fragrance of wholeness and victory. You can trust God with your YES!

CPSIA information can be obtained
at www.ICGtesting.com
Printed in the USA
BVOW03s0155070917
494151BV00001B/4/P